Nature's Children

WASPS

Jen Green

GROLIER
EDUCATIONAL

FACTS IN BRIEF

Classification of Wasps

Class:	*Insecta* (insects)
Order:	*Hymenoptera* (wasps, bees, and ants)
Family:	There are about 60 families of wasps.
Species:	There are over 100,000 species of wasps.

World distribution.　Worldwide, except in the polar regions.

Habitat.　Varies according to species, from tropical rain forests to temperate woodlands and meadows, even deserts.

Distinctive physical characteristics.　Tiny to large insects with two sets of wings; body colors are usually bright; yellow and black or red and black stripes are often present; females of many species have a sting at the tip of the abdomen.

Habits.　About 10 percent of species are social wasps, living in large groups. The rest are solitary or parasitic wasps.

Diet.　Adults feed on sugary liquids such as nectar, rotting fruit, or sap. Most larvae are meat eaters, although some feed on plants.

© 1999 Brown Partworks Limited
Printed and bound in U.S.A.
Editor: James Kinchen
Designer: Tim Brown

Published by:

GROLIER
EDUCATIONAL

**Sherman Turnpike, Danbury,
Connecticut 06816**

Library of Congress Cataloging-in-Publishing Data
Wasps.
　　p. cm. -- (Nature's children. Set 6)
　　ISBN 0-7172-9371-8 (alk. paper) -- ISBN 0-7172-9351-3 (set)
　　1. Wasps--Juvenile Literature. [1. Wasps.] I. Grolier Educational (Firm) II. Series.

QL535.2G74 1999
595.79'8—dc21
　　　　　　　　　　　　　　　　　　　　　　　　　　　　98-33406

Contents

What is the world's scariest animal? Ask many people what animal they fear most, and it would not be a large, ferocious hunter such as a lion or tiger, but a little wasp. With their yellow and black bodies, wasps are well known as fierce fighters and feared for their stings. It's true that wasps can be a menace in late summer, when they wander in search of sweet foods. They may end up in your can of soda or making a bee line for your ice cream! Yet not all wasps can sting, and wasps are also very helpful. They aid farmers by eating insect pests that harm their crops. They help flowers to make seeds and grow. Wasps make good mothers too—they go to a lot of trouble to get food for their young. In fact, wasps are amazing creatures. Read on to find out more.

A wasp hunts for ripe blackberries.

See-Through Wings

So what are wasps? Wasps are insects, like beetles, ants, and butterflies. You can tell insects from other bugs by counting their legs. Adult insects are the only bugs with six legs. Bodies of grown-up insects have three sections: the head, the thorax, or middle section, and the abdomen at the rear.

There are many thousands of different species, or types, of insects in the world. To help identify them, they are divided into large groups called orders. Wasps are members of an order called Hymenoptera. The name means "transparent wing," and true to their name, wasps have two sets of see-through wings. Bees and ants are closely related to wasps and belong to the same family.

A mason wasp shows off its three body sections. Like most wasps, it has a narrow "waist" between its thorax and abdomen.

The World of Wasps

Would you be surprised to hear that there are 100,000 different kinds of wasps in the world? Not all have yellow and black striped bodies. Some are red and black, shiny blue, or green in color. Wasps vary in size, too. Some are tinier than the period at the end of this sentence. At the other end of the scale is the tarantula hawk wasp, the largest stinging insect in the world, which can grow to two and a half inches (six centimeters) long.

Wasps are found in most parts of the world, from hot, dry deserts to lush tropical rain forests. Some species live in meadows. Others prefer woodlands or cool forests. Most wasps live on their own. But some species, called social wasps, live in large, well-organized societies. Every species has different habits, and no two kinds live in exactly the same way.

This brightly colored cuckoo wasp
is feeding on poinsettia flowers.

Inside and Out

Do you know where your skeleton is? Like most large animals, the bones that form our skeletons are inside our bodies. The outside of our bodies is covered with soft skin. Wasps and other insects are built the other way around. Their bodies are protected by a hard case on the outside. The case protects the soft parts inside like a little suit of armor. The case is tough and light like plastic, not heavy like metal armor.

All living things, including wasps, need oxygen from the air to breathe. Insects do not have lungs to take in air, as we do. Instead, tiny openings in their body cases allow air to pass inside.

A wasp searches for nectar deep inside a flower.

Changing Shape

Have you ever been told you look like your mom or dad? Whether or not we closely resemble our parents, all human children look a lot like adults, only smaller.

Insects are very different from us, and many young insects, including wasps, look nothing like their parents. During their lives they go through four separate stages.

A wasp starts off life as an egg, which hatches out into a wingless grub, or larva. With no legs or eyes, the delicate, milky-white larva can barely move. All the food it needs is provided by its mother, so all it has to do is eat! Each time it gets bigger, it breaks out of its old, hard skin and reveals a new, larger one underneath. When the larva reaches full size, it sheds its skin for the last time and becomes a pupa. The hard, brown pupa seems lifeless, but inside the young wasp is not resting, it is changing. Finally it emerges in a completely different form—as an adult wasp. This amazing process is called metamorphosis, which means "changing shape."

Opposite page: About a week after becoming a pupa, an adult German wasp emerges from its cell.

13

Amazing Antennae

The world of a little wasp is very different from our own. The grassy lawn under our feet is a great jungle to a wasp, with stalks of grass towering high into the air. A daisy open in the sunshine is a spacious landing pad. An apple on the grass is the size of a hot-air balloon.

Because of the difference in scale wasps do not sense the world as we do. Their world is mainly made up of smells and tastes. A wasp's main sensing tools are its antennae, or feelers, found on the head. These can be used to smell, taste, and touch. A wasp's head and body are covered with little hairs that can pick up the vibrations made by sounds. These hairs can also tell the wasp how cold or hot it is.

A fallen apple is a feast for wasps.

Beady Eyes

In addition to smell, feel, and taste, wasps can also see well, and they have more than just two eyes. On top of its head a wasp has three tiny eyes, called simple eyes, arranged in a triangle. These cannot focus, but they can see light and dark. The wasp also has two large eyes, called compound eyes, made of many lenses. Each lens sees a small part of the surroundings, and the wasp's brain fits these fragments together to make a larger picture, like a mosaic made of little pieces.

The wasp's compound eyes cover most of its head. Because of this, it can see in front, behind, and above, all at the same time! Wasps are very good at sensing the smallest movement. If the movement spells danger, the wasp can quickly fly away.

With five eyes and large, powerful jaws, the German wasp is a deadly hunter of small bugs and grubs.

Armed and Dangerous

The first thing that we learn about wasps is to beware of their stings. The stinger is a sharp spine at the tip of the insect's rear. It is connected to a sac of venom in the abdomen. When the wasp stings, the spine punctures the skin. Then venom is pumped into the wound from the sac. Ouch—that hurts!

Wasps use their stings for different reasons. Wasps may sting to defend themselves or to protect their nest. Or they may sting to kill or paralyze prey animals, often other insects, to feed their young.

Not all wasps can sting. In those that can, the stinger has developed from the part that is used to lay eggs, so only females can sting.

Without stingers, male wasps are not much use as hunters. In social wasp species a few males, called drones, live inside the nest. Many kinds of solitary wasps have no males at all; the females can lay eggs without mating.

A spider wasp uses its sting to paralyze a wolf spider, but it must be careful—the spider has a powerful venom of its own.

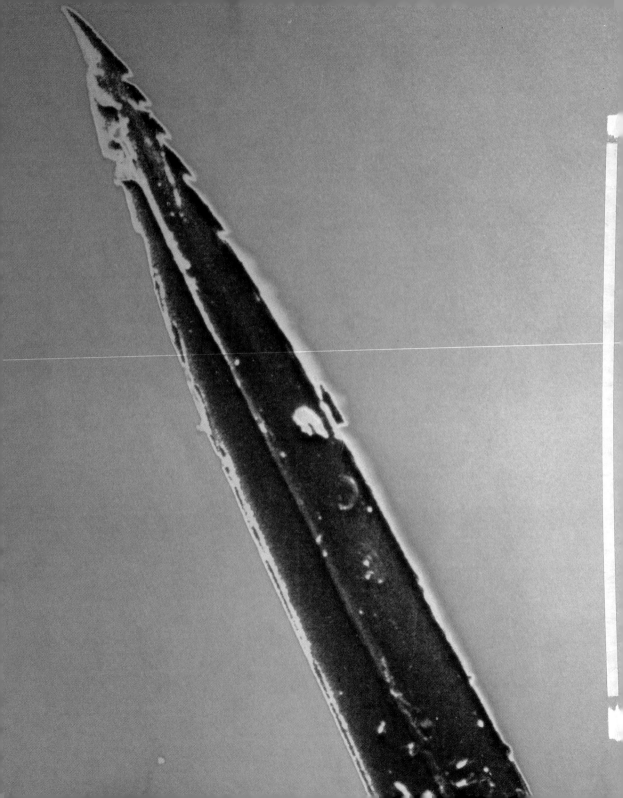

Sharp Stings

Have you ever been stung by a wasp? Usually a wasp sting is not a danger to people, but it is still a painful experience. Wasps can remove their stinger from the wound after stinging, unlike bees, which have barbed stingers that cannot be withdrawn. The sting will hurt less if you give the wasp enough time to remove it. However, in the heat of the moment this is easier said than done!

If a wasp has left its stinger in your skin, it can be taken out with tweezers—but take care not to squeeze the venom sac, which may be left attached to the end of the spine. Clean out the wound with antiseptic. A cool, damp cloth will ease the pain. Normally a wasp will only sting to defend itself. If you keep calm and still, a wasp will usually mind its own business and move away.

A wasp stinger magnified 530 times. Venom flows down the groove in the middle of the spine.

Keep Away

Have you seen yellow and black striped markings on construction sites or along the edges of stairs? These colors warn that there is danger and tell us to watch our step.

Yellow, red, and black are warning colors that were invented by animals. Creatures such as wasps and deadly snakes wear these colors to show that they are dangerous. Many animals have green, brown, or mottled coats. These help their owners to hide among leaves, grass, or soil. Warning colors have the opposite effect—they shout "Notice me!"

Other animals understand warning colors and know they should keep away. So wasps are well protected by their stripes. Some other insects, such as hoverflies, cannot sting but look just like wasps. This tricks other animals; they think that the hoverfly is a wasp and leave it alone.

A hoverfly's wasp-like markings trick birds and other enemies into leaving it alone.

A New Colony

Most wasps lead solitary lives, but some kinds, such as common wasps and hornets (yellow jackets), live in large groups known as colonies. The colony is founded in spring by a fertile female wasp, called a queen. The queen carefully selects a location for her nest. She prefers a sheltered, quiet spot with room for expansion. Often she chooses to live under the eaves of a house or in a tree, although some queens prefer underground burrows.

To start her nest, the queen gathers dry wood fibers from a fallen branch or wooden post. She gnaws at the fibers, leaving little grooves in the wood. Then she chews the fibers to soften them and molds them into a cup-shaped nest. Like a little lampshade, the nest hangs from a tree branch or wooden rafter by a slender stalk. Inside the nest the queen builds a comb of six-sided cells and lays an egg in each.

A queen wasp at work on her nest.

The Next Generation

Inside their cells the eggs hatch into larvae. The small, white grubs have no legs or wings, so they are helpless. They hang down inside the comb and wait to be fed. These children will one day be her workers, so the queen tends them carefully. She hunts the larvae of other insects and chews them into pieces to feed her young.

On this rich diet the grubs grow quickly. Soon they are ready to pupate. Each grub spins a cap of silk to close its cell. Inside it turns into a pupa. In about a week it emerges as an adult wasp. These new worker wasps are female but cannot lay eggs. Instead, they take over the work of finding food and making the nest bigger. The queen is free to concentrate on laying more eggs.

The wasp larvae grow quickly on the rich diet provided for them by their mothers.

At the White House

Have you ever made papier-mache? You tear paper into strips and mix it with water until it forms a pulp. Paper seems a flimsy material, but when it dries out, papier-mache is as strong and solid as rock!

The nests of social wasps are made of strong paper pulp, like papier-mache. Nests are pale brown, gray, or white in color, depending on the type of wood the wasps use to make the pulp. The workers enlarge the nest all summer, and it can grow to the size of a soccer ball. The outside is protected by a tough envelope of paper layers. At the bottom is the entrance, where busy workers fly in and out all day. The nest has many floors, like a multistory building. Each has a comb of cells in which new wasps are growing. The floors are connected by passageways, so the workers can visit every cell.

Busy tree wasp workers fly in and out of the nest entrance.

Wasp City

The wasp colony is like a town. All citizens have their own jobs to do. Some wasps are hunters. They fly in search of insect food and bring it back to nurses, who feed and tend the grubs. Cleaner wasps clear out garbage and keep the nest spick and span. As each cell is vacated by a new worker, it is cleaned out and made ready for the queen to lay another egg.

Some wasps are builders, adding new floors to the nest. They measure the distance between the paper walls with their antennae to make sure the nest grows evenly. Other wasps are guards, keeping watch and ready to defend their home. In hot weather they fan the nest with their wings to keep the larvae cool.

Teamwork

The key to the smooth running of the nest is teamwork. The queen is the team captain. She controls the workers by producing special chemical smells. These are passed between the workers so everyone knows what to do.

By summer the nest may contain as many as 500 cells and house 2,000 workers. Early in the fall it is time to prepare for next year's colony. The workers build new, large cells in the comb. The grubs that hatch there are given extra food and develop into young queens and drones. These young wasps fly from the nest and mate. The young queens must find a way to survive the winter so that they can start new colonies in spring.

Surviving Winter

Like all insects, wasps are cold-blooded creatures. Unlike your body, which stays warm all the time, a wasp's body can be warm or cold, depending on the temperature of its surroundings. When their bodies are cold, wasps cannot be active or move around. After a chilly summer night they bask in the sunshine until they are warm enough to go about their business.

As winter approaches, the weather gets too cold for wasps to be active. The workers and drones die off, and only the young queens are left. Each queen finds a snug place such as a woodpile or garden shed and hides there. She survives the winter in a deep sleep called hibernation. In spring she wakes up and flies away to found a new wasp city.

A common wasp queen sleeps through the winter hidden in a woodpile.

Amazing Nests

Not all social wasps build round, paper nests. Some species use different materials or build nests with weird and wonderful shapes. In South America some wasps build their nest from mud, not paper. The mud is very heavy, so the nest is built around a strong tree branch that can support the weight.

Other South American wasps build a nest that is pricklier than a porcupine. They cover the outside with sharp paper spines. The prickly cover is so hard that the nest can last for 30 years.

Some wasps build open nests with no outer cover to protect the grubs inside. Instead, the nursery cells are surrounded by special guard cells, like a ring of sentry boxes. Inside each cell is a wasp sentry, on the lookout and ready to scent danger. The guards will use their stingers if an enemy comes too close.

Opposite page: *These wasps from the Amazon rain forest are beating their bodies against the outside of the nest. This makes a loud drumming noise that scares intruders away.*

A Lonely Life

Many kinds of wasps do not live in a colony but are loners. Some build a little nest just for their young. These small homes are even more varied than the large nests built by social wasps. Female sand and digger wasps make a little burrow in the soil. Potter wasps build tiny clay pots, either underground or hanging from a twig.

A wasp single mom goes to a lot of trouble to stock her nest with food. She hunts down caterpillars, spiders, or other bugs but does not kill them. Instead, she stings her victims to paralyze them, so they cannot move. Then she drags the victims' bodies back to her nest, lays her eggs, and seals the entrance. When the wasp grubs hatch out, they have a handy living larder of meat.

A potter wasp stocks her nest with a paralyzed caterpillar.

Plant Homes

Next time you go for a walk in the fall, you may spot a pink, wispy ball of "moss" on a wild rose bush. The wispy ball is known as a rose pincushion. It is a growth, called a gall, made by the plant. The growth is caused by a tiny gall wasp, which lays its eggs on the rose bud. The plant reacts by growing wispy tissue around the grubs. The pincushion makes a safe home where the grubs can hide from enemies. They feed on the bud until they are ready to change into adults and fly away.

Other gall wasps produce different galls on trees and shrubs. On an oak tree the small, brown "fruits" hanging from twigs and the little buttons under the leaves are both galls produced by wasps.

A rose pincushion gall on a wild rose bush.

Fresh Meat

Some wasps make no home at all, either for themselves or for their young. Instead, they lay their eggs directly onto a slow-moving insect such as a caterpillar. When the eggs hatch, the wasp grubs feast on fresh caterpillar meat until they pupate. The caterpillar is eaten alive. It only dies when the wasp larvae become adults.

This way of life sounds gruesome. But the mother wasp is only doing her best to keep her young alive and well. These wasps, called parasites, help farmers by killing large numbers of pesky insects that harm their crops. Some farmers even introduce the wasps to kill pests, rather than spraying their fields with chemicals.

The braconid wasp lays her eggs on slow-moving aphids.

Keen Tracker

Wood wasps are the string beans of the wasp world. They have long, slim bodies, and females have long stingers like fine needles. These mother wasps have an amazing skill that they use to feed their young. They lay their eggs on the grubs of beetles that live inside tree trunks. Normally the beetle grubs are safe inside the wood. Unfortunately for them, however, the wood wasp can somehow sense their movements beneath the bark. She bores into the trunk with her stinger and lays her eggs on their bodies. When they hatch, the young wasps feed on the beetle grubs.

No one understands how the wood wasp tracks down her victims hiding in the wood. But wasps are full of surprises and mysteries, and we still have lots to learn about them.

The great wood wasp's slender stinger is strong enough to penetrate even the hardest wood.

The Friendly Wasp

You may not feel friendly toward wasps if one comes buzzing around your picnic. Yet wasps can be our great friends. In spring and summer wasps help farmers and gardeners by hunting caterpillars that eat crops and vegetables. They are also friends of many plants, which produce beautiful flowers just to attract them.

To make seeds, many plants must be fertilized by powdery pollen. Wasps and bees help by carrying pollen from one flower to another. It happens like this: wasps visit flowers to sip their sugary nectar. As they reach into the flower to collect nectar, their bodies get dusted with the plant's pollen. When they visit another flower, the pollen rubs off to fertilize the second plant, so it can make seeds. Without wasps and other insects there would be fewer flowers to brighten our homes and gardens.

Words to Know

Abdomen The rear part of an insect's body that contains the stomach and parts used to lay eggs.

Colony Group of animals that live together.

Drone Male wasp or bee.

Fertile Able to produce young after mating.

Gall A swelling produced by a plant when an insect lays its eggs on it.

Larva Young insect. The larvae of some insects can also be called grubs, maggots, or caterpillars.

Lens Part of an animal's eye that helps it to see.

Mosaic Picture made up of many small, colored tiles.

Nectar Sweet liquid found in flowers, drunk by insects such as butterflies, bees, and wasps.

Parasite Animal that lives on or in another animal and gets its food from it.

Pupa An insect that is changing from a larva to an adult inside a hard case.

Thorax The middle part of an insect's body that holds the wings and legs.

INDEX

Cover Photo: Stephen Dalton / NHPA
Photo Credits: Stephen Dalton / NHPA, pages 4, 15, 23, 28, 40, 44; Anthony Bannister;
ABPL / Corbis, page 7; Anthony Bannister / NHPA, pages 8, 39; Gary Braasch / Corbis, page
11; ANT Photo Library / NHPA, pages 12, 16, 19, 27, 32; Ron Boardman; Frank Lane Picture
Agency / Corbis, page 20; Joe McDonald / Corbis, page 24; G. I. Bernard / NHPA, page 35;
Michael Fogden and Patricia Fogden / Corbis, page 36; N. A. Callow / NHPA, page 43.